Dialing Desire: Breaking Free from Phone Sex Addiction

Dialing Desire: Breaking Free from Phone Sex Addiction

Breaking Free from Phone Sex Addiction

Charles Allan

Better than Bonkers

CONTENTS

CONTENTS

Legal Disclaimer:
The information provided herein is intended for general informational purposes only and does not constitute professional advice, diagnosis, or treatment for addiction issues. It is crucial to recognize that addiction is a complex and nuanced condition, and individual circumstances may vary.

The content provided does not replace the expertise, judgment, or guidance of qualified professionals such as licensed therapists, counselors, or medical practitioners. Individuals dealing with addiction issues are strongly encouraged to seek the assistance of trained and certified professionals who can provide personalized assessments and tailored recommendations based on their unique situations.

This information is not intended to create, and receipt or viewing does not constitute, a professional-client relationship. The transmission and receipt of information contained on this platform, in whole or in part, or communication via the internet, email, or any other means do not constitute or create a therapeutic or counseling relationship between the user and the content provider or OpenAI.

Furthermore, OpenAI and the content provider disclaim any and all liability for any loss or damage incurred as a direct or indirect result of the use, application, or interpretation of the information presented. Reliance on any information provided herein is solely at the user's own risk.

If you or someone you know is struggling with addiction issues, it is imperative to consult with a qualified professional promptly. Delaying or avoiding seeking professional help may exacerbate the condition and impede the recovery process.

Always consult with a licensed professional before making any decisions or taking any actions regarding your addiction issues. Legal and ethical considerations may vary across jurisdictions, and professional advice is necessary to ensure compliance with applicable laws and regulations.

In summary, the information provided serves as a general resource and should not be construed as a substitute for professional advice. OpenAI and the content provider expressly disclaim any responsibility for actions taken or not taken based on the information presented. Individuals are urged to consult with qualified professionals for accurate assessments and guidance tailored to their specific circumstances.

First Printing, 2024

ISBN: 979-8-8690-8229-9
EISBN: 979-8-8690-8230-5

Understanding Sex Addiction

Expanding on the Definition of Sex Addiction:

Sex addiction is a multifaceted and intricate condition that transcends mere compulsive behavior, delving into the realms of psychology, relationships, and personal well-being. This captivating yet perplexing phenomenon grips individuals in an unrelenting cycle of intense sexual thoughts, fantasies, and behaviors, defying attempts at restraint despite the ensuing negative consequences. Beyond the contours of conventional sexual desire, sex addiction evolves into a compulsive and all-encompassing force, casting a pervasive shadow over various facets of one's life.

Within the intricate tapestry of sex addiction, distinct niches emerge, each with its unique set of challenges. Online sex addiction, for instance, unfolds in the digital landscape, where individuals succumb to the allure of cybersex, pornography, and explicit online conversations. Meanwhile, the labyrinth of porn addiction weaves a narrative centered on the relentless consumption of explicit content, fostering distorted perceptions of sexuality and fostering unrealistic expectations.

In the expansive landscape of sex addiction, cybersex addiction emerges as a distinctive subtype, entailing virtual sexual encounters through platforms like chat rooms, webcams, and various online forums. Simultaneously, variations like compulsive masturbation, prostitution addiction, exhibitionism addiction, voyeurism addiction, and phone sex addiction introduce nuanced expressions of the overarching theme — an uncontrollable compulsion to engage in diverse sexual behaviors.

Navigating the intricate dynamics of sexual addiction within relationships presents a particularly arduous challenge. The clandestine nature of sexual activities outside committed partnerships, commonly seen in infidelity and cheating, becomes a crucible for emotional pain, trust erosion, and, at times, the dissolution of relationships.

Understanding the nuanced and comprehensive definition of sex addiction is paramount for individuals grappling with these issues. This understanding serves as a validating compass, guiding them toward seeking appropriate support and embarking on a journey to reclaim control over their lives. It is imperative to emphasize that sex addiction is a treatable condition; armed with the right interventions, individuals can liberate themselves from its grasp, fostering personal growth and restored well-being.

Delving Deeper into Different Types of Sexual Addictions:

Sexual addiction, an intricate tapestry woven into the fabric of human experiences, manifests in various forms, affecting individuals across diverse backgrounds. In this exploration, we unravel the diverse threads that compose the intricate patterns of sexual addiction, offering insight into the behaviors and patterns that contribute to an insatiable yearning for sexual gratification.

In the digital age, online sex addiction and porn addiction emerge as dominant forces, fueled by the unfettered access to explicit content on the internet. Individuals find themselves ensnared in the labyrinth of compulsive viewing, navigating a treacherous landscape marked by strained relationships, diminished productivity, and emotional detachment.

Cybersex addiction, another pervasive form, takes root in the virtual realm, where individuals immerse themselves in online platforms for virtual sexual encounters, explicit chat rooms, and forums.

This addiction exacts a toll on personal and professional spheres, fostering isolation, diminishing self-esteem, and distorting perceptions of healthy sexual relationships.

Compulsive masturbation, a formidable manifestation of sexual addiction, entails an overpowering urge to indulge in excessive self-pleasure. This all-consuming behavior begets physical discomfort, strains relationships, and diminishes satisfaction in real-life sexual encounters.

Prostitution addiction, a distinctive facet, compels individuals towards compulsive engagement with sex workers, leading to severe legal and health repercussions. Meanwhile, exhibitionism addiction, voyeurism addiction, and phone sex addiction present their unique patterns, each a distinct expression of the relentless urge for sexual gratification.

Sexual addiction within relationships unveils an intricate dance of dependence, wherein individuals seek solace in clandestine sexual encounters beyond committed partnerships. This form of addiction, marked by guilt, shame, and eroding trust, challenges the very foundations of intimate connections.

Understanding the diverse landscape of sexual addictions is instrumental for those grappling with these challenges. Armed with awareness, individuals can navigate their unique struggles and embark on a path towards healing, be it through therapy, support groups, or specialized treatment programs. Breaking free from the shackles of sexual addiction is a journey paved with self-discovery and resilience, offering the promise of restored control and the cultivation of healthier, more fulfilling relationships.

Exploring the Impact of Sex Addiction on Relationships:

Within the intricate tapestry of human connection, sex addiction emerges as a formidable force capable of leaving indelible marks on relationships. Whether manifesting as online sex addiction, porn addiction, or cybersex addiction, the consequences reverberate through the lives of both the addict and their significant other.

For those ensnared by the allure of addictive behaviors, the commitment to relationships often succumbs to the magnetic pull of indulgence. This can birth a myriad of problems, from infidelity and emotional detachment to the erosion of trust. As the addict becomes consumed by their compulsions, the partner's emotional and physical needs languish unmet, casting a pall over the relationship and nurturing seeds of betrayal, anger, and hurt.

The complexities deepen for those who succumb to infidelity driven by sex addiction. The compulsive need for sexual gratification outside committed relationships initiates a destructive cycle of lies, deceit, and potential relationship implosion. The accompanying guilt and shame become potent catalysts for straining the bond between partners, making the reconstruction of trust and intimacy an uphill battle.

Sexual addiction within relationships unfurls in varied expressions. Compulsive masturbation, prostitution addiction, exhibitionism addiction, voyeurism addiction, and phone sex addiction represent diverse manifestations, each inflicting its unique set of consequences upon both the addict and their partner.

Crucially, seeking help becomes an imperative for both the sex addict and their significant other. Therapy, counseling, and support groups offer a sanctuary for addressing underlying issues fueling the addiction, providing a platform to rebuild trust and intimacy within the relationship. The crucible of open and honest communication emerges as an indispensable tool for both parties to heal, forging a path toward a healthier, more fulfilling partnership.

In this exploration of sex addiction's impact on relationships, the intricacies of consequences are laid bare. By shedding light on these effects and offering guidance on navigating this challenging terrain, a roadmap is forged for individuals grappling with sex addiction, porn addiction, or any other form of sexual addiction. This journey beckons towards breaking free from destructive patterns and cultivating relationships steeped in health, love, and understanding.

Recognizing the Signs and Symptoms of Sex Addiction:

Within the labyrinth of human experiences, sex addiction lurks as a complex and often misunderstood condition, exerting profound impacts on individuals and their relationships. In this exploration, we venture into the realm of signs and symptoms, seeking to illuminate the shadows of this pervasive issue and empower individuals to identify if they are entangled in its web.

A hallmark sign of sex addiction lies in the relentless preoccupation with sexual thoughts, fantasies, or behaviors — an obsession that transcends daily life activities. The resulting disruption manifests as an inability to focus on anything beyond the realm of one's sexual desires, leading to excessive engagement in behaviors such as watching pornography, seeking escort services, or immersing oneself in cybersex.

A dangerous escalation unfolds with an increasing tolerance to sexual stimuli. Individuals find themselves trapped in a cycle where more intense or frequent experiences become imperative to satiate their cravings, propelling them into a perilous spiral of escalating behaviors in pursuit of the elusive satisfaction.

A loss of control becomes a defining symptom, as individuals repeatedly grapple with attempts to curtail or cease their sexual behaviors, only to succumb to the unrelenting urge. This lack of control births a maelstrom of guilt, shame, and distress, further entwining them in the clutches of their addiction.

The consequences of sex addiction reverberate through relationships, with infidelity and cheating becoming common manifestations that jeopardize trust and intimacy. Financial strain may also manifest, as individuals funnel substantial resources into their addictive behaviors.

Sex addiction, devoid of gender, age, or sexual orientation limitations, can afflict anyone. The pivotal first step toward recovery lies in recognizing these signs and symptoms. For those resonating with this exploration, the consideration of seeking professional help or joining specialized support groups becomes a beacon of hope.

The upcoming chapters promise a deeper dive into effective strategies and techniques for breaking free from the clutches of phone sex addiction, empowering individuals to reclaim control over their lives. Remember, the acknowledgment of signs and symptoms marks the genesis of the journey toward recovery, and you are not alone in traversing this path.

2

Exploring Online Sex Addiction

Introduction:

As the digital era continues to shape our lives in unprecedented ways, the impact of technology on our most intimate experiences has become undeniable. While the internet has facilitated knowledge-sharing and connectivity, it has also paved the way for a concerning phenomenon: the rise of online sex addiction. In this subchapter of "Dialing Desire: Breaking Free from Phone Sex Addiction," we embark on an exploration of the alarming ascent of online sex addiction, dissecting its intricate impacts on individuals, relationships, and the fabric of society.

The Transformative Power of Technology:

Advancements in technology have not only enhanced our lives but have also revolutionized the landscape of human sexuality. The internet, with its accessibility and anonymity, has given rise to a spectrum of behaviors falling under the umbrella of online sex addiction, encompassing cybersex addiction, compulsive masturbation, pornography addiction, and more. In this subchapter, we unravel the complexities of sexual addiction in the digital age, where the boundaries between the real and virtual worlds blur.

Deciphering the Mechanics:

The allure of easily accessible explicit content, coupled with virtual platforms for sexual interaction and the enticing veil of anonymity, has fueled the rapid proliferation of online sex addiction. We navigate through the intricate web spun by these addictive behaviors, exploring the psychological, emotional, and physical consequences that individuals grapple with as they navigate the laby-rinth of online sex addiction.

Impact on Relationships:

For those entangled in committed relation-ships, the implications of online sex addiction are profound. We delve into the intricate dynamics of sexual addiction within relationships, dissect-ing how it corrodes trust, contributes to infidelity, and fractures the emotional bonds that under-pin healthy partnerships. This exploration aims to provide guidance for individuals seeking to navi-gate and heal from the tumult caused by online sex addiction in their relationships.

Unmasking Prostitution and Exhibitionism:

Online platforms have not only facilitated sexual interactions but have also streamlined the darker aspects of online sex addiction, notably prostitution and exhibitionism. This subchapter unearths the exploitative nature of these activities and scrutinizes the repercussions they impose on both individuals and society at large.

Charting the Path to Freedom:

Our exploration culminates in a discussion on the journey to recovery from online sex addiction. Practical strategies, resources, and insights are offered for sex addicts, phone addicts, and those engaged in infidelity, empowering them to break free from the shackles of online sex addiction. Emphasis is placed on the importance of seeking professional help, constructing a robust support network, and implementing healthy coping mechanisms to regain control over one's life and relationships.

Conclusion:

"The Rise of Online Sex Addiction" exposes the potent and destructive fusion of technology with sexual addiction. By shedding light on the multifaceted manifestations of online sex addiction and providing guidance for recovery, this subchapter strives to assist individuals in breaking free from the chains of their addictions, restoring damaged relationships, and forging a healthier, more fulfilling path forward.

Navigating the Intersection of Technology and Sex Addiction:

In the contemporary digital landscape, technology acts as a pivotal force shaping various dimensions of our lives, including our intimate experiences. The accessibility and anonymity afforded by the internet and smartphones have ushered in new avenues for sexual exploration and expression. However, for individuals grappling with sex addiction, these technological advancements can become a double-edged sword.

Online sex addiction, porn addiction, cybersex addiction, and other related compulsive behaviors have burgeoned in our society, leveraging the ease of access to explicit content and the virtual realms of sexual gratification. This exploration delves into the nuanced interplay between technology and sex addiction, unraveling the mechanisms that propel individuals into a perilous cycle of addictive behaviors.

The Role of Instant Gratification:
One of the primary catalysts for the symbiosis

between technology and sex addiction is the allure of instant gratification. With a mere tap on a screen or a click of a mouse, individuals can plunge into a vast sea of sexual content or virtual encounters, all without leaving the confines of their own homes. This instantaneous reward can create a reinforcing loop, intensifying the compulsive behavior and fostering a loss of control.

The Anonymity Paradox:

The anonymity afforded by technology serves as a double-edged sword in the realm of sex addiction. While providing a sense of detachment from real-life consequences, online platforms also become breeding grounds for the exploration of deep-seated desires without fear of judgment. This detachment, however, can lead to a dissociation from reality, blurring the boundaries between the virtual and the tangible and fueling addictive behaviors.

Risks in Relationship Dynamics:

For those entangled in relationships, technology poses significant risks. Sexting, online affairs, and virtual sexual encounters can erode trust, inti-macy, and emotional connection within partner-ships. The consequences of these activities extend beyond the digital realm, causing real-world strain, guilt, shame, and betrayal.

Recognizing Technology's Role in Addiction:
Understanding the pivotal role of technology in fueling sex addiction is crucial for those striv-ing to break free from its clutches. By deciphering the triggers, patterns, and consequences associated with online sex addiction, individuals gain insight into their addictive behaviors, paving the way for informed and empowered recovery.

A Balancing Act:
While technology serves as an enabler of ad-dictive behaviors, it also harbors the potential for healing and recovery. Online support groups, ther-apy apps, and educational resources can serve as invaluable tools for individuals seeking help for sex addiction. The goal is to harness technology's positive aspects in the journey toward recovery,

utilizing it as a force for self-discovery, connection, and healthier sexual navigation.

In conclusion, technology's influence on human sexuality is a multifaceted landscape, offering both opportunities and pitfalls. Understanding the intricate dance between technology and sex addiction is paramount for individuals seeking liberation from the cyclic grip of addiction, ushering in a phase of reclamation of a healthy and fulfilling sexual well-being.

Exploring the Perils of Online Sexual Activities:

This subchapter embarks on an exploration of the various perils entwined with engaging in online sexual activities. As the digital age evolves, the allure of virtual encounters and explicit content has become more accessible than ever. However, for individuals grappling with sex addiction, porn addiction, or those cheating on their significant others, it is imperative to comprehend the potential risks and repercussions associated with these behaviors.

The Menace of Addiction:

Chief among the dangers of online sexual activities is the insidious development of addiction. Engaging in cybersex, compulsive masturbation, or phone sex can give rise to a dependence on these activities for sexual gratification. This addictive spiral permeates an individual's time, energy, and focus, casting a dark shadow on personal relationships, work performance, and overall well-being.

Distorted Perceptions:

Online sexual activities have the power to create a distorted perception of reality. Porn addiction, for instance, can foster unrealistic expectations and dissatisfaction with real-life sexual encounters, straining intimate relationships and contributing to infidelity as individuals seek to fulfill their desires outside committed partnerships.

Cyber Risks:

Partaking in online sexual activities exposes

individuals to potential cyber threats. The sharing of explicit content or interaction with unknown individuals can make one vulnerable to blackmail, identity theft, or the dissemination of personal information. Moreover, engaging with illegal platforms or sex workers brings the added risk of legal consequences and potential harm.

Psychological Toll:

The psychological impact of online sexual activities is profound. Voyeurism addiction, exhibitionism addiction, and prostitution addiction can induce feelings of guilt, shame, and low self-esteem. The secretive nature of these activities creates a cycle of guilt and isolation, adversely affecting an individual's mental health and overall quality of life.

Relationship Strain:

For those in committed relationships, engaging in online sexual activities can be particularly damaging. Sexual addiction within relationships can lead to shattered trust, emotional distress, and the erosion of intimacy. Cyber-infidelity can be as devastating as physical cheating, inflicting immense pain on both partners.

Recognizing and Confronting the Dangers:
Understanding and acknowledging these dangers is the critical first step toward breaking free from phone sex addiction and other online sexual behaviors. By seeking professional help, individuals can develop healthier coping mechanisms, rebuild relationships, and regain control over their lives.

Addressing the root causes of these addictive behaviors and seeking support from therapists, support groups, or specialized treatment centers are crucial steps toward recovery. Armed with the right tools and guidance, individuals can overcome their online sexual addictions, forging a path toward fulfillment in healthier, more authentic connections.

Strategies for Liberation from Online Sex Addiction:
In the current digital age, the internet unfolds a

realm of possibilities and instant gratification. Yet, for individuals entangled in the web of online sex addiction, the easy access to explicit content, cybersex, and pornography can quickly spiral out of control, wreaking havoc on their personal lives and relationships. Fear not – there is hope for recovery. This subchapter unravels effective strategies to aid individuals in breaking free from the clutches of online sex addiction.

1. Cultivate Awareness and Acceptance:

The inaugural step toward overcoming any addiction is the recognition and acceptance of the problem. It's crucial to acknowledge that online sex habits have veered into problematic territory and commit to initiating change.

2. Seek Professional Guidance:

Connecting with a qualified therapist or counselor experienced in treating sexual addiction is imperative. They can serve as guides through the recovery process, offering support and aiding in the development of coping mechanisms.

3. Set Clear Boundaries:

Establishing clear boundaries and instituting

rules around internet usage are paramount. Utilizing internet filters, parental controls, or software designed to restrict access to adult websites can limit exposure to explicit content.

4. Substitute Negative Habits:

Engage in alternative activities that provide a healthy outlet for sexual energy. Exploring hobbies, regular exercise, or joining support groups where individuals facing similar challenges connect can redirect focus and energy positively.

5. Foster Healthy Relationships:

Building strong, intimate connections with partners or significant others is vital for overcoming online sex addiction. Open communication about struggles and collaborative efforts to rebuild trust and intimacy are crucial components of the recovery process.

6. Embrace Mindfulness and Self-Control:

Develop the practice of being present in the moment, recognizing triggers that lead to online sex addiction. Employ mindfulness techniques to redirect thoughts and focus on positive aspects of life.

7. Create a Support Network:

Surround oneself with an understanding and supportive network of individuals who can offer encouragement and accountability. Joining a support group or seeking guidance from a sponsor can provide invaluable assistance.

Remember, the journey to overcoming online sex addiction demands commitment, patience, and self-compassion. By implementing these strategies and seeking professional help, individuals can reclaim control over their lives, heal damaged relationships, and rediscover a healthy and fulfilling sexual well-being.

3

Confronting Porn Addiction

Understanding the Power of Pornography and Its Impact on Individuals

The pervasive influence of pornography in our modern society cannot be overstated, especially when examining its role in various forms of sexual addiction. In this comprehensive subchapter, we strive to illuminate the profound impact that pornography has on individuals entangled in the destructive cycle of addiction. By delving into the underlying mechanisms and psychological dynamics at play, we aim to empower those grappling with sex addiction, porn addiction, and infidelity with the knowledge necessary to break free from these addictive behaviors.

At its core, pornography exploits the brain's reward system, triggering the release of dopamine, a neurotransmitter associated with pleasure and motivation. This powerful chemical reaction creates a cycle of craving and reward, compelling individuals to seek increasing levels of stimulation. Over time, this tolerance to the effects of pornography can lead addicts to search for more extreme forms of sexual content, resulting in severe consequences for personal relationships and overall mental well-being.

For those struggling with sex addiction, online sex addiction, porn addiction, and cybersex addiction, pornography often serves as a primary trigger for their compulsive behaviors. The internet's accessibility and anonymity provide fertile ground for the development and reinforcement of addictive patterns. Similarly, individuals dealing with compulsive masturbation, prostitution addiction, exhibitionism addiction, voyeurism addiction, phone sex addiction, and sexual addiction in relationships are intimately acquainted with the allure of pornography. It can act as a catalyst for acting out desires in real life or exacerbate existing addictive behaviors.

Moreover, pornography has the potential to distort one's perception of intimacy and relationships. By presenting unrealistic and idealized portrayals of sexuality, it can create expectations that are impossible to meet in real-life encounters, leading to dissatisfaction and strained relationships. This distortion often contributes to infidelity, perpetuating a cycle of guilt and shame for those who cheat on their significant others.

Understanding the power of pornography is a crucial step for individuals seeking to break free from their addictive behaviors. Recognizing the neurological and psychological impact it has enables individuals to begin developing strategies and coping mechanisms to overcome their addiction. This may involve seeking professional help, engaging in therapy, or joining support groups that provide a safe space for recovery.

In conclusion, pornography exerts significant influence over individuals struggling with various forms of sexual addiction. Its ability to exploit the brain's reward system and distort perceptions of intimacy makes it a formidable adversary in the battle against addiction. However, armed with knowledge, support, and a determination to change, individuals can break free from the grip of pornography addiction and reclaim their lives.

The Far-Reaching Effects of Porn Addiction on Mental and Emotional Well-being

In the contemporary digital age, where explicit content is readily accessible, the effects of porn addiction on mental and emotional health cannot be underestimated. In this comprehensive sub-chapter, we delve into the profound impact that prolonged exposure to pornography can have on individuals grappling with addiction, as well as on relationships affected by this behavior.

For individuals dealing with sex addiction, porn addiction often acts as a gateway to further compulsive behaviors. Continuous consumption of explicit material can lead to desensitization to sexual stimuli, diminishing the ability to experience intimacy and pleasure in real-life relationships. This detachment from reality can result in feelings of loneliness, depression, and isolation.

Similarly, for individuals who cheat on their significant others, porn addiction can exacerbate their infidelity. The unrealistic expectations and fantasies perpetuated by pornography can create an insatiable desire for novelty and variety, leading to a constant search for new sexual experiences outside the committed relationship. The guilt, shame, and secrecy associated with infidelity can further deteriorate the mental and emotional well-being of those involved.

Furthermore, the niches of sex addiction, online

sex addiction, and cybersex addiction are closely intertwined with porn addiction. The ease of accessing online sexual content, engaging in cybersex activities, or indulging in compulsive masturbation can intensify the addictive cycle. This excessive reliance on virtual interactions can lead to social withdrawal, relationship conflicts, and a distorted perception of healthy sexuality.

Moreover, the detrimental effects of porn addiction extend beyond personal relationships. Those suffering from prostitution addiction, exhibitionism addiction, voyeurism addiction, and phone sex addiction often rely on pornography as a means to fuel their compulsions. The constant exposure to explicit material can reinforce deviant behaviors, perpetuating a destructive cycle that erodes mental and emotional well-being.

In conclusion, the effects of porn addiction on mental and emotional health are far-reaching and devastating. For sex addicts, porn addiction can hinder the ability to form intimate connections. For those who cheat, it can amplify infidelity and destroy trust. The various niches of sex addiction are closely intertwined with porn addiction, exacerbating the addictive cycle. It is crucial for individuals struggling with these issues to recognize the detrimental impact of their addiction and seek professional help. Through therapy, support groups, and a commitment to recovery, individuals can break free from the grasp of porn addiction and regain control over their mental and emotional well-being.

Breaking Free from the Grip of Porn Addiction: A Comprehensive Guide

In this in-depth subchapter, we embark on an exploration of the gripping world of porn addiction, aiming to provide a comprehensive guide for those seeking effective strategies to break free from its clutches. Whether one identifies as a sex addict, porn addict, or an individual who cheats on their significant other, this chapter is tailored to offer valuable insights and guidance in overcoming this challenging addiction.

Porn addiction is a pervasive issue affecting individuals across various niches, from online sex addiction to compulsive masturbation and prostitution addiction. The constant accessibility and anonymity provided by the internet have made it easier than ever to indulge in cybersex addiction, voyeurism addiction, and exhibitionism addiction.

Recognizing that a problem exists is the initial step toward breaking free from porn addiction. It takes courage and self-awareness to acknowledge the detrimental effects it can have on relationships, mental health, and overall well-being. In this sub-chapter, we guide individuals through the process of self-reflection and provide practical tools to help overcome this addiction.

Understanding the root causes of addiction is crucial to developing effective coping mechanisms. We delve into the underlying emotional triggers that may drive reliance on pornography and explore techniques for managing stress, anxiety, and loneliness without resorting to harmful behaviors.

We also emphasize the importance of seeking professional help and joining support groups to gain necessary guidance and encouragement from others who have successfully overcome similar addictions. Connecting with individuals who share these struggles can provide solace and motivation, affirming that one is not alone in the journey toward recovery.

Furthermore, we explore the role of healthy relationships in overcoming porn addiction. Nurturing open and honest communication with a partner is essential for rebuilding trust and fostering intimacy. Practical tips for addressing this sensitive topic and rebuilding a fulfilling and healthy sexual relationship are provided.

Breaking free from the grip of porn addiction is a challenging process that requires commitment, self-reflection, and a support system. This subchapter aims to equip individuals with the necessary tools and resources to embark on a journey toward a healthier, more fulfilling life. Recovery is possible, and individuals deserve to break free from the shackles of addiction.

Rebuilding Intimacy and Connection in Relationships After Sexual Addiction

In the fast-paced digital age we live in, many individuals find themselves grappling with various forms of sexual addiction, including online sex addiction, porn addiction, cybersex addiction, and phone sex addiction. These addictions often lead to destructive behaviors such as infidelity and dishonesty, severely damaging the intimacy and connection within relationships. However, hope exists for those willing to confront their addiction and actively work toward rebuilding trust and intimacy.

This comprehensive subchapter explores the crucial steps that sex addicts, porn addicts, and those who cheat on their significant others must take to rebuild intimacy and connection within their relationships. Whether struggling with compulsive masturbation, prostitution addiction, exhibitionism addiction, voyeurism addiction, or any form of sexual addiction in relationships, the principles discussed here will be applicable to the journey.

First and foremost, acknowledging and taking responsibility for one's actions is vital. Recognizing the negative impact addiction has had on a relationship is the initial step toward change. It is essential to communicate honestly with a partner, expressing remorse and a sincere desire to rebuild the trust that has been shattered.

Next, a commitment to therapy and support groups is crucial. Seeking professional help from therapists who specialize in sexual addiction is highly recommended. These experts can guide individuals through understanding the root causes of addiction, developing healthy coping mechanisms, and reestablishing healthy boundaries within a relationship.

Rebuilding intimacy and connection also requires open and honest communication with a partner. This means actively listening to their needs, fears, and concerns while sharing one's own feelings and struggles. Rebuilding trust takes time, patience, and consistent effort, but with the right support system and a willingness to change, it is possible to heal and restore the intimacy that was lost.

In addition to therapy and communication, establishing new healthy habits and routines is essential. This may include setting boundaries in one's digital life, practicing self-care, and finding alternative outlets for stress and emotional release. By replacing destructive behaviors with positive and healthy ones, individuals can rebuild intimacy and connection within their relationships.

Remember, rebuilding intimacy and connection in relationships after sexual addiction is a challenging but achievable goal. By taking responsibility, seeking professional help, communicating openly, and developing healthy habits, individuals can break free from the cycle of addiction and create a stronger, more fulfilling relationship based on trust, intimacy, and connection.

4

Overcoming Cybersex Addiction

Navigating the Temptations of Cybersex and its Vast Repercussions in the Digital Era

As we traverse the realms of the digital age, the allure of cybersex has evolved into an increasingly formidable challenge for individuals entangled in various forms of sexual addiction. The amalgamation of easy access, inherent anonymity, and an unending reservoir of explicit content renders cybersex an enticing outlet for those yearning for sexual gratification. However, delving into the realm of cybersex does not come without severe consequences, as it has the potential to wreak havoc not only on personal relationships but also on the intricate fabric of one's mental well-being.

For individuals grappling with the throes of sex addiction, the allure of cybersex lies in its ability to offer an instantaneous escape from reality. The virtual world, with its perceived safety, becomes a sanctuary where individuals can explore the depths of their desires without the looming specter of judgment or rejection. The addictive nature of cybersex finds its roots in the release of dopamine, a neurotransmitter intricately linked with pleasure and reward. This release is triggered by the perpetual novelty and excitement embedded in online sexual encounters.

Yet, the consequences of succumbing to the allure of cybersex can be profoundly devastating. In committed relationships, it frequently metamorphoses into a catalyst for infidelity, acting as a corrosive agent that eats away at the foundations of trust. The labyrinth of secrecy and deception woven into the maintenance of online sexual relationships has the potential to erode the emotional bonds between partners, giving rise to feelings of betrayal, anger, and resentment.

Furthermore, the unrestrained consumption of cybersex content has the potential to desensitize individuals to real-life intimacy, impairing their ability to form authentic connections. The constant exposure to explicit material might warp one's perception of healthy sexual relationships, fostering unrealistic expectations. This distortion, in turn, can breed dissatisfaction with real-life partners and plunge individuals into a ceaseless cycle of seeking more extreme forms of online sexual stimulation.

Beyond the emotional toll, the repercussions of cybersex addiction can extend into the financial realm. Many individuals find themselves ensnared in the spending of exorbitant amounts on paid online sexual services, leading to financial instability and, in extreme cases, potential bankruptcy. The addictive nature of cybersex often renders self-control elusive, spelling dire consequences for personal and financial well-being.

Escaping the magnetic allure of cybersex demands a multi-faceted approach. Seeking professional assistance from therapists specializing in sex
addiction stands as an invaluable cornerstone, providing guidance and support. Active involvement
in support groups and connection with others who
have triumphed over similar challenges can provide
solace and motivation. Developing healthier coping mechanisms, such as engaging in physical activities, pursuing hobbies, and fostering improved
communication within relationships, serves to redirect energy away from cybersex and toward more
wholesome outlets.

In conclusion, the magnetic allure of cybersex
remains a perpetual temptation for those ensnared
by sex addiction. However, the repercussions of
succumbing to this virtual world are severe, with
the potential to annihilate personal relationships,
induce financial instability, and compromise overall well-being. Acknowledging these dangers and
seeking professional help are pivotal steps in ex-
tricating oneself from the clutches of cybersex

addiction, paving the way toward reclaiming a life that is healthier and more fulfilling.

Delving into the Psyche: Unraveling the Complexities of Cybersex Addiction in the Digital Epoch

In the epoch of ubiquitous technology, where the digital realm permeates every facet of our existence, the emergence of new forms of addiction is an unsurprising development. One such addiction that has garnered significant attention is cybersex addiction. This subchapter undertakes the intricate task of unraveling the psychological factors that contribute to this addictive behavior, shedding light on the complexities of a phenomenon that continues to gain prominence in the digital landscape.

Cybersex addiction, characterized by compulsive engagement in sexual activities through online platforms such as chat rooms, webcams, or virtual reality, is fueled by a confluence of psychological factors deeply rooted in an individual's psyche.

Anonymity and the allure of fantasy emerge as pivotal factors behind cybersex addiction. The online world offers a perceived detachment from reality, empowering individuals to create alter egos and participate in sexual scenarios that may never find expression in their real lives. This escape into the virtual realm serves as a temporary reprieve from stress, loneliness, or other emotional struggles, making it an attractive outlet for those seeking emotional fulfillment.

Moreover, cybersex addiction often finds its roots in underlying psychological issues, such as low self-esteem, depression, or anxiety. Individuals may deploy cybersex as a coping mechanism, providing a shield to escape their insecurities or mask emotional pain. The virtual world, with its promises of feeling desired, accepted, and in control, offers a refuge, if only temporarily.

The accessibility and ease of access to online sexual content further contribute to the addictive nature of cybersex. With just a few clicks, individuals can access a vast array of explicit material, reinforcing their desire for instant gratification. This continual availability of sexual stimuli can disrupt the brain's reward circuitry, fostering a cycle of craving and compulsive behavior.

For individuals ensnared in sex addiction, phone addiction, or infidelity, cybersex addiction can unleash devastating consequences on their relationships. The veil of secrecy and deception inherent in this addiction acts as a corrosive force, eroding trust and intimacy and leading to fractured bonds and shattered lives.

Understanding the psychological factors behind cybersex addiction is paramount for addressing and overcoming this destructive behavior. By identifying the underlying emotional issues and providing alternative coping strategies, individuals can break free from the grip of addiction, reclaiming control over their lives and relationships.

In the subsequent chapters, we will embark on an exploration of effective treatment approaches and strategies to aid individuals in combating cyber-sex addiction. Through avenues of self-reflection, supportive networks, and professional guidance, recovery becomes a tangible prospect for those ensnared in the clutches of cybersex addiction.

5

Tackling Compulsive Masturbation

The Intricate Dynamics of the Compulsive Nature of Masturbation in Our Hyper-Connected World

In the midst of today's hyper-connected world, where technology seamlessly infiltrates every facet of our lives, it should come as no surprise that our sexual behaviors, too, have undergone a transformation. A behavior that has taken center stage, often with alarming prevalence, is the compulsive nature of masturbation. Within the confines of this subchapter, we embark on an in-depth exploration of the multifaceted factors that contribute to this addictive behavior, aiming to unravel its complexity and providing insights into strategies for breaking free from its formidable grip.

Masturbation, widely acknowledged as a natural and healthy sexual expression, can, for some individuals, evolve into an all-consuming compulsion. This phenomenon isn't isolated but rather interwoven with other niche addictions such as online sex addiction, cybersex addiction, and even prostitution addiction, creating a complex web of intertwined behaviors.

The primary driving force behind compulsive masturbation finds its roots in the accessibility and anonymity afforded by the internet. The explosion of online sex addiction and porn addiction, with their boundless supply of explicit content just a click away, creates a relentless cycle. Individuals find themselves ensnared in an unending quest for the next dopamine-driven high, perpetuating the compulsive behavior.

Moreover, the compulsion thrives on the thrill

of secrecy and voyeurism. Those entangled in this behavior often derive pleasure from observing others engaged in sexual activities, whether through online platforms or in person. This exhibitionism and voyeurism addiction further fuels the compulsion, as individuals become fixated on seeking out new experiences to satiate their insatiable desires.

In the realm of committed relationships, the impact of compulsive masturbation extends beyond the individual, wreaking havoc on intimacy and trust. It becomes an escape from authentic connections, fostering infidelity and leading to a breakdown of emotional bonds. Navigating sexual addiction within relationships demands open communication, therapeutic intervention, and a steadfast commitment to rebuilding trust.

The journey of breaking free from the grip of compulsive masturbation is undoubtedly challenging, yet far from insurmountable. The crucial first step involves recognizing the problem and acknowledging the need for recovery. Seeking professional help from therapists specializing in sexual addiction becomes paramount. These professionals can offer not only guidance and support but also tailored strategies to navigate the intricate landscape of compulsive behavior.

Additionally, integrating healthy coping mechanisms and uncovering alternative outlets for sexual energy is imperative. Activities such as exercise, creative pursuits, and social engagement serve as effective tools to redirect focus away from compulsive tendencies. Establishing a robust support network, comprising understanding individuals who have faced similar challenges, provides invaluable encouragement along this transformative journey.

In conclusion, the compulsive nature of masturbation emerges as a significant concern in our contemporary digital age. For individuals grappling with sex addiction, porn addiction, or those veering into infidelity, the cycle of self-indulgence becomes a pervasive force that detrimentally impacts relationships and overall well-being. Nevertheless, armed with the right support, strategic interventions, and an unwavering commitment to change, breaking free from this addiction becomes an attainable goal, heralding the prospect of reclaiming a life that is both healthy and fulfilling.

The Far-reaching Implications of Compulsive Masturbation on Physical and Mental Well-being

Compulsive masturbation, often entwined with various forms of sexual addiction like online sex addiction, porn addiction, cybersex addiction, and phone sex addiction, extends its tendrils into the realm of physical and mental health. In this subchapter, "The Impact of Compulsive Masturbation on Physical and Mental Health," we navigate through the intricate landscape of consequences that this behavior imposes on individuals grappling with sex addiction, porn addiction, and infidelity.

Physical Health Consequences:
The ramifications of compulsive masturbation on physical health transcend the immediate, potentially leading to enduring problems. Excessive engagement in this behavior can result in genital

soreness, irritation, and, in severe cases, injuries. Normal sexual functioning may be disrupted, manifesting as difficulties in achieving orgasm or maintaining an erection. Furthermore, individuals entrenched in compulsive masturbation may inadvertently neglect their physical well-being, fostering poor dietary habits, inadequate exercise, and disrupted sleep patterns, contributing to an overall decline in physical health.

Mental Health Consequences:

The impact on mental health is profound for those grappling with sex addiction, porn addiction, and infidelity. Feelings of guilt, shame, and diminished self-esteem often accompany the constant pursuit of sexual gratification. The obsessive nature of the behavior gives rise to intrusive thoughts, heightened anxiety, and, in some cases, depression, all of which collectively cast a shadow over an individual's overall quality of life. Compulsive masturbation also poses a threat to the ability to form and sustain healthy relationships, as it transforms into a substitute for authentic connection and intimacy.

Relationship Consequences:

Compulsive masturbation's devastating conse-quences extend into the realm of intimate rela-tionships. Partners of individuals struggling with sex addiction or infidelity grapple with feelings of betrayal, inadequacy, and sorrow. The erosion of trust, breakdown in communication, and strained relationships become apparent. The obsessive focus on self-pleasure can lead to a neglect of the part-ner's emotional and sexual needs, exacerbating the damage to the relationship.

Seeking Help and Recovery:

Acknowledging the profound impact of com-pulsive masturbation on physical and mental health marks a pivotal step towards recovery. Individuals entrenched in sex addiction, porn addiction, and infidelity should actively seek professional help and consider joining support groups tailored to sexual addiction. Therapeutic interventions can provide valuable insights into the root causes of compulsive behavior and assist in developing healthy coping mechanisms.

In conclusion, compulsive masturbation unfurls a tapestry of physical and mental health consequences for individuals ensnared in sex addiction, porn addiction, and infidelity. Understanding the detrimental effects of this behavior sets the stage for proactive steps towards recovery, healing relationships, and reclaiming control over one's life.

6

Addressing Prostitution Addiction

Exploring the Nuances of Prostitution Addiction: A Comprehensive Examination

Prostitution addiction, a deeply ingrained and multifaceted concern, resonates across the globe, impacting countless individuals. This subchapter undertakes the ambitious task of unraveling the intricacies of this addiction, casting a spotlight on its origins, repercussions, and potential routes to recovery. Whether one identifies as a sex addict, a porn addict, engages in infidelity, or is merely intrigued by the complexities of prostitution addiction, this chapter offers profound insights into the subject matter.

Prostitution addiction, colloquially known as sex work addiction, manifests as an uncontrollable compulsion to partake in paid sexual activities. Its roots delve into an array of underlying factors, such as childhood trauma, low self-esteem, and a distorted sense of intimacy. The allure of immediate gratification and the deceptive semblance of control further amplify the addictive nature of this behavior.

A pivotal complexity of prostitution addiction lies in the nebulous space between consent and exploitation. While some willingly embrace sex work as a means of survival or personal choice, countless others find themselves ensnared, coerced, manipulated, or trapped in the industry against their will. Understanding these nuances is imperative in addressing the root causes of this addiction and offering tailored support to those grappling with its impact.

Prostitution addiction, beyond its toll on individuals, extends its tendrils into the realm of relationships. Infidelity, veiled in secrecy, and emotional detachment become prevalent themes, corroding trust and intimacy within partnerships. The ceaseless pursuit of novel sexual experiences sets the stage for a perilous cycle of risk-taking behaviors, imperiling personal safety and overall well-being.

Recovery from prostitution addiction, while undeniably arduous, remains a feasible journey. A holistic approach, addressing the emotional, psychological, and social facets contributing to the addiction, is paramount. Therapy, support groups, and rehabilitation programs specialized for sex addiction furnish the requisite tools and guidance for those yearning to break free from the clutches of this addiction.

By shedding light on the intricacies of prostitution addiction, this subchapter aspires to instill understanding and empathy among sex addicts, porn addicts, and individuals entangled in infidelity. It serves as a poignant reminder that addiction is a malady, not a moral failing, and that with the right support and commitment, recovery is not only conceivable but achievable.

Ultimately, our collective aim is to empower individuals to discern the destructive patterns of their behavior, encourage them to seek help, and guide them on a transformative journey toward healing, self-discovery, and the cultivation of healthier relationships. Together, we possess the capacity to shatter the chains of prostitution addiction and reclaim our lives.

The Profound Emotional Odyssey of Prostitution Addiction

Prostitution addiction, a deeply intricate issue, exacts a hefty emotional toll on those ensnared by its clutches. In this subchapter, we embark on an expedition to uncover the emotional dimensions accompanying this form of addiction, shedding light on the internal struggles faced by sex addicts, phone sex addicts, and individuals who grapple with infidelity.

Beyond the transactional act itself, prostitution addiction often emanates from underlying emotional anguish, trauma, or a dire need for validation. Those ensnared in this addiction grapple with profound feelings of guilt, shame, and self-loathing. The clandestine nature of their activities fuels a perpetual fear of exposure, engendering heightened anxiety and stress.

A pivotal facet of the emotional toll exacted by prostitution addiction lies in the erosion of healthy relationships. Individuals engaged in infidelity not only betray the trust of their partners but also inflict damage upon their own emotional well-being. The associated guilt and shame set in motion a vicious cycle of addictive behavior, intensifying emotional distress.

For those entangled in phone sex or online sexual encounters, the emotional toll is equally profound. The ceaseless quest for validation and sexual stimulation through virtual interactions begets feelings of isolation and detachment from real-life relationships. Phone sex addiction, cybersex addiction, and compulsive masturbation collectively contribute to a distorted perception of intimacy, impeding the formation of genuine connections with others.

Prostitution addiction also inflicts damage on self-esteem and self-worth. Relying on paid sexual encounters for validation begets a diminished sense of self, fostering the belief that one's worth hinges solely on their capacity to fulfill sexual desires. This skewed perspective perpetuates the addiction cycle and intensifies emotional turmoil.

Moreover, individuals grappling with prostitution addiction often grapple with legal consequences, introducing an additional layer of stress and emotional strain. The looming fear of apprehension or facing criminal charges compounds feelings of guilt, shame, and anxiety.

In conclusion, the emotional toll of prostitution

addiction stands as an imposing force. It not only impacts the individuals mired in this addiction but also reverberates through their relationships, self-esteem, and overall well-being. Recognition and addressal of the emotional aspects prove instrumental in breaking free from the clutches of this addiction, fostering healthier avenues to fulfill emotional needs, and establishing genuine connections with others.

Navigating the Path to Healing: Seeking Help for Prostitution Addiction

In the realm of addiction, the pivotal step toward recovery lies in seeking help and support. Prostitution addiction, akin to various forms of sexual addiction, casts a devastating shadow on individuals and their relationships. This subchapter embarks on an exploration of the significance of seeking help and support specifically for prostitution addiction, elucidating how this endeavor can pave the way for liberation from the destructive cycle.

Prostitution addiction, a complex tapestry woven from compulsive engagement in sexual activities with sex workers, frequently emanates from deep-seated emotional and psychological factors. Trauma, low self-esteem, and a dire need for validation and control weave a narrative that entraps individuals in a seemingly interminable cycle, rendering them powerless to overcome their destructive behaviors.

The acknowledgment of the need for help marks the genesis of recovery. It demands courage to recognize the existence of a problem, but seeking professional help becomes an imperative step in regaining control over one's life. Therapists and counselors specializing in sex addiction offer a safe and non-judgmental haven, allowing individuals to explore the underlying issues contributing to their addiction.

Support groups, exemplified by entities like Sex Addicts Anonymous (SAA), emerge as crucial allies in the journey to recovery. These groups create a platform for individuals to share experiences, garner support from others who have walked similar paths, and absorb insights from collective wisdom. The connection with fellow individuals navigating the challenges of prostitution addiction bestows a sense of comfort and empowerment.

In addition to professional help and support groups, it becomes paramount for individuals to foster open and honest communication with their significant others. Prostitution addiction often begets infidelity and dishonesty within relationships. Seeking the understanding and support of a partner constitutes a vital component of the recovery journey. Couples therapy or relationship counseling can play a pivotal role in rebuilding trust, improving communication, and establishing a supportive environment for healing.

The emancipation from prostitution addiction demands dedication, commitment, and a willingness to delve into the underlying issues fueling this destructive behavior. By seeking help and support, individuals acquire the tools and strategies necessary to surmount this addiction and construct healthier, more fulfilling lives.

In conclusion, seeking help and support stands as a crucial juncture for individuals wrestling with prostitution addiction. Professional therapy, support groups, and transparent communication within relationships converge to sculpt a trajectory toward successful recovery. Remember, the path to liberation exists, and seeking support constitutes the beacon illuminating the way out of the cycle of prostitution addiction.

Rediscovering Self-Worth and Nurturing Healthy Connections: A Path to Liberation from Phone Sex Addiction

In our collective odyssey to break free from the clutches of phone sex addiction, our focus converges on addressing the underlying issues that have orchestrated our descent into this destructive abyss. A crucial facet of the recovery process centers around the revitalization of our self-worth and the cultivation of healthy relationships. Through these endeavors, we chart a course to regain control over our lives and pave the way for a future imbued with fulfillment.

Sex addiction, whether manifested through online sex, porn, cybersex, or other compulsive behaviors, often finds its roots in a deficiency of self-esteem and an insatiable need for validation. The initiation of the recovery journey necessitates an acknowledgment of this fact, prompting us to embark on the process of rebuilding our self-worth. It is imperative to comprehend that our intrinsic worth transcends the realm of our sexual behaviors or the approval of others. Each individual possesses inherent value, deserving of love, respect, and the pursuit of healthy relationships.

The rekindling of our self-worth mandates a commitment to self-reflection and self-care. This journey may involve engaging in therapeutic practices, journaling, embracing mindfulness, or exploring various forms of self-expression such as art, music, or physical activities. By investing time and energy into our personal growth, we lay the foundation for a robust self-perception, learning to appreciate our worth beyond the confines of our sexual behaviors.

In tandem with the reconstruction of self-worth, the establishment of healthy relationships emerges as a pivotal aspect of the recovery journey. For those entangled in destructive behaviors like infidelity, rebuilding trust and fostering wholesome connections may appear daunting, yet it remains a tangible goal with dedication and a willingness to embrace change.

Honesty and transparency stand as bedrocks in this process. Open communication serves as the cornerstone for rebuilding trust and fostering understanding. Seeking professional help, if necessary, becomes an invaluable resource, as therapists offer guidance and support throughout the intricate process of rebuilding relationships.

Setting boundaries, both for oneself and respecting those of others, emerges as another vital component. Establishing healthy boundaries ensures that both parties feel secure and valued within the relationship. Healthy relationships, predicated on mutual respect, trust, and consent, serve as the fertile ground for personal and shared growth.

Lastly, surrounding oneself with a supportive community catapults the recovery journey into a realm of shared understanding and empowerment. Participation in support groups or online forums tailored to sex addiction or relationships affords individuals the opportunity to connect with others who have weathered similar storms, providing invaluable insights, encouragement, and a sense of belonging.

The twin pursuits of rediscovering self-worth and establishing healthy relationships act as fundamental steps along the path to recovery from phone sex addiction. By confronting the underlying issues, investing in self-care, and fostering open and honest connections, we liberate ourselves from the shackles of destructive patterns, ushering in a life marked by fulfillment and balance. Remember, the inherent worth of every individual encompasses love, respect, and the potential for thriving relationships.

7

Confronting Exhibitionism Addiction

Unraveling the Complex Dynamics of Exhibitionism Addiction: An In-Depth Exploration

Exhibitionism addiction, a multifaceted and frequently misconstrued facet of sexual addiction, remains shrouded in complexity. Within this sub-chapter, our intent is to illuminate the nuances surrounding this specific addiction, delving into its motivations and the underlying factors that contribute to its genesis. Armed with a profound comprehension of exhibitionism addiction, individuals grappling with this issue, as well as those entangled in sex addiction, porn addiction, and infidelity, can embark on a journey to address and surmount their addictive behaviors.

The labyrinth of exhibitionism addiction intricately weaves a compulsive need to expose one's genitals or engage in sexual acts in public or semi-public settings. This behavior often seeks arousal and validation through the shock or surprise of unsuspecting viewers. While the motivations behind exhibitionism addiction may differ from person to person, clinical research has unearthed several common themes that underpin this intricate issue.

For some, exhibitionism serves as a coping mechanism, offering an ephemeral respite from emotional pain or stress. The act of exposing oneself in public becomes a momentary distraction or an adrenaline-fueled escape, momentarily eclipsing underlying issues. Additionally, certain individuals may turn to exhibitionism to validate their self-worth or elevate their self-esteem. The attention and arousal garnered from onlookers become a transient remedy for feelings of inadequacy or low self-confidence.

A significant driving force behind exhibitionism addiction is the quest for power and control. Engaging in exhibitionistic acts allows individuals to wield dominance over others, providing a semblance of control in their lives. This desire for power often emanates from feelings of powerlessness or a lack of control in other realms, such as relationships or the professional sphere.

Moreover, exhibitionism addiction can intertwine with voyeuristic tendencies. Some individuals derive pleasure from witnessing the reactions of others as they expose themselves, thereby fueling a destructive cycle where exhibitionism and voyeurism become intertwined components, each satisfying the other's sexual cravings.

Understanding the motivations behind exhibitionism addiction proves pivotal for those seeking recovery. By identifying the underlying emotional issues, traumas, or insecurities propelling this behavior, individuals can commence the process of addressing these root causes. Therapeutic interventions, participation in support groups, and self-reflection exercises form integral components of this process, offering individuals the necessary tools and coping mechanisms to liberate themselves from the clutches of exhibitionism addiction.

In conclusion, exhibitionism addiction stands as a multifaceted dimension of sexual addiction that warrants comprehensive understanding for effective intervention. By delving into the motivations behind this addiction, individuals ensnared in exhibitionism, as well as those grappling with sex addiction, porn addiction, and infidelity, can initiate a transformative journey of self-discovery and healing, ultimately breaking free from the destructive cycle of their addictive behaviors.

Navigating Legal and Social Waters: The Repercussions of Exhibitionism

Exhibitionism, manifesting as a form of sexual

addiction involving the intentional exposure of one's genitals or sexual acts in public, carries profound legal and social consequences for those embroiled in its grasp. Within this subchapter, we embark on an exploration of the potential ramifications of exhibitionism and its impact on both the individual and the broader social fabric.

From a legal standpoint, exhibitionism positions itself as a criminal offense across numerous jurisdictions. Laws against public indecency categorically condemn the deliberate exposure of one's genitals in public spaces, encompassing the realm of exhibitionism. Depending on the jurisdiction and the specific circumstances, individuals found participating in exhibitionism may encounter penalties ranging from fines, probation, and community service to the stark reality of imprisonment. Adding another layer of gravity, individuals may be compelled to register as sex offenders, a designation with enduring consequences for both personal and professional aspects of their lives.

Beyond the rigid framework of legality,

exhibitionism unleashes social repercussions with considerable force. The engagement in such behavior can inflict damage upon personal relationships, particularly in the context of committed partnerships. The revelation of exhibitionist activities becomes a catalyst for emotions of betrayal, fractured trust, and emotional trauma for the partner, potentially culminating in the demise of the relationship.

Simultaneously, exhibitionism casts its shadow on an individual's standing within their community or professional spheres. As the knowledge of such behavior becomes public, stigma, social isolation, and, in severe cases, job loss may ensue. The embarrassment and shame entwined with exhibitionism contribute to a compromised self-esteem, exacerbating feelings of guilt and further exacerbating the social consequences.

For those grappling with exhibitionism, seeking professional help stands as a critical juncture for addressing their addictive behaviors. Therapy, counseling, and engagement in support groups collectively supply the necessary tools to comprehend and manage the underlying causes of exhibitionism. By tackling these root causes, individuals can work towards breaking free from the clutches of their addiction and avoiding the dire legal and social consequences associated with exhibitionism.

In conclusion, the exhibitionism spectrum unfurls severe legal and social consequences for individuals ensnared in its web. It is imperative for those grappling with this addiction to actively seek help and support, not only to overcome their compulsions but also to navigate and mitigate the potential fallout of their actions. By unearthing and addressing the underlying issues propelling exhibitionism, individuals can forge a path towards a life that is healthier and more fulfilling, liberated from the legal and social shackles associated with this behavior.

Therapeutic Odyssey: Navigating the

Maze of Exhibitionism Addiction Recovery

Exhibitionism addiction, a intricate and often misconstrued facet of sexual addiction, calls for a nuanced and strategic therapeutic approach. This form of addiction, characterized by an intense and compulsive urge to expose oneself in public settings, necessitates a comprehensive exploration of therapeutic methodologies. In this subchapter, we will embark on an odyssey to unearth various therapeutic approaches that can facilitate the journey to liberation for individuals grappling with exhibitionism addiction, empowering them to regain control over their lives.

Cognitive-behavioral therapy (CBT) emerges as a cornerstone in the therapeutic repertoire for exhibitionism addiction. CBT places its focal point on identifying and challenging the distorted thoughts and beliefs that propel addictive behavior. Through structured sessions with a trained therapist, individuals delve into recognizing triggers and develop healthier coping mechanisms to supplant the urge for exhibitionism. CBT, in its comprehensive scope, also aids individuals in exploring the underlying emotional issues that serve as the bedrock of their addiction, such as low self-esteem or unresolved trauma.

Group therapy, another promising therapeutic avenue, provides a nurturing and non-judgmental space where individuals can share their experiences, struggles, and triumphs with others who intimately understand their addiction. Through these collective discussions, individuals gain insights into their behavior, receive constructive feedback from peers, and draw from the collective wisdom of shared experiences. Group therapy cultivates a sense of accountability, fostering commitment to the recovery journey.

Simultaneously, individual therapy emerges as a beneficial modality for those wrestling with exhibitionism addiction. Individual therapy affords more personalized attention, honing in on the specific underlying causes and triggers unique to each individual. Therapists may employ techniques such as psychodynamic therapy or trauma-focused therapy to plumb the depths of addiction roots, providing tailor-made treatment plans for individualized care.

In certain scenarios, medication may complement therapeutic interventions, offering support to manage underlying mental health conditions connected to exhibitionism addiction, such as anxiety or depression. When integrated with therapy, medication can contribute to stabilizing mood, curbing cravings, and fortifying overall recovery efforts.

Crucially, surmounting exhibitionism addiction demands unwavering commitment to long-term recovery and sustained support. Support groups like Sex Addicts Anonymous or SMART Recovery prove invaluable, offering ongoing support and strategies for relapse prevention.

In conclusion, exhibitionism addiction, with its profound repercussions on lives and relationships, necessitates a strategic therapeutic approach. Through methodologies such as cognitive-behavioral therapy, group therapy, individual therapy, and judicious use of medication, individuals can extricate themselves from the clutches of exhibitionism addiction, steering toward recovery and rebuilding their lives. Through sustained support and a commitment to the recovery journey, individuals can reconstruct their lives and cultivate healthy, fulfilling relationships.

8

Breaking Free from Phone Sex Addiction

The Proliferation and Pitfalls of Phone Sex Addiction in the Digital Era

In our contemporary digital landscape, the magnetism of phone sex addiction has surged, ensnaring individuals from diverse backgrounds. Whether one grapples with sex addiction, porn addiction, or the complexities of infidelity, the realm of phone sex promises an alluring escape from reality. Yet, beneath its surface allure lies a multitude of perils capable of wreaking havoc on personal relationships and mental well-being.

Phone sex addiction stands as a subset of online sex addiction, encompassing various forms of sexual behavior facilitated through digital platforms. The allure lies in the convenience and anonymity it offers, making it particularly appealing to those seeking instant gratification. The capacity to connect with like-minded individuals at any time, from the sanctuary of one's home, exerts a seductive pull.

For sex addicts, phone sex addiction presents an outlet to explore their deepest desires without the tangible repercussions often accompanying traditional sexual encounters. The act of engaging in cybersex or succumbing to compulsive masturbation yields a transient sense of pleasure and release, momentarily eclipsing emotional turmoil or stress.

However, the dangers woven into the fabric of phone sex addiction cannot be dismissed. The relentless pursuit of sexual gratification through this medium can distort perceptions of intimacy and genuine relationships. It has the potential to foster unrealistic expectations, hindering individuals from forming authentic emotional connections and ensnaring them in a cycle of unsatisfying encounters.

Moreover, the ramifications of phone sex addiction extend to existing relationships. Engaging in phone sex as a form of infidelity can erode trust and intimacy, potentially causing irreparable damage. The secretive nature of this addiction often leads to strained relationships, accompanied by feelings of guilt and a breakdown in communication.

Financial implications further compound the issue. Frequent use of paid phone sex services or involvement with online platforms that charge for explicit content can lead to significant financial strain, intensifying the emotional toll of addiction.

It is imperative for individuals grappling with phone sex addiction to recognize the urgency of seeking help. Therapy and support groups dedicated to sexual addiction provide a safe haven to address the underlying issues propelling this behavior. Developing healthy coping mechanisms, fostering open communication, and rebuilding trust in relationships become vital steps towards overcoming phone sex addiction.

In conclusion, while the appeal of phone sex addiction may be undeniable in our technologically advanced era, it is paramount to acknowledge the inherent dangers it poses to personal relationships, mental health, and financial stability. By acknowledging these destructive consequences and actively seeking professional help, individuals can emancipate themselves from the clutches of phone sex addiction, regaining control over their lives.

Unveiling the Deep-Rooted Causes of Phone Sex Addiction: An In-Depth Exploration

In this digital age, where technology acts as an expansive canvas for exploration and connection, it is no surprise that various forms of addictive behaviors have sprouted. One such addiction, often residing in the shadows of recognition and understanding, is phone sex addiction. In the subchapter titled "Unveiling the Deep-Rooted Causes of Phone Sex Addiction," we embark on a profound exploration of the underlying factors that contribute to this compulsive behavior, providing nuanced insights and guidance for those ensnared by this addiction.

Phone sex addiction, akin to other forms of sexual addiction, casts its shadow across individuals from all walks of life. Whether one grapples with sex addiction, porn addiction, or finds themselves entangled in the complexities of infidelity, understanding the root causes that fuel this behavior becomes paramount. This knowledge serves as the compass guiding individuals on the journey to emancipation from the grip of phone sex addiction.

This subchapter intricately navigates the various niches of sexual addiction—online sex addiction, porn addiction, cybersex addiction, compulsive masturbation, prostitution addiction, exhibitionism addiction, voyeurism addiction, and sexual addiction within relationships. By dissecting these niches, our aim is to provide a comprehensive understanding of the multifaceted factors that contribute to phone sex addiction and how they interweave with other addictive behaviors.

Through a tapestry woven with personal narratives, expert insights, and scientific research, "Unveiling the Deep-Rooted Causes of Phone Sex Addiction" seeks to unearth the underlying psychological, emotional, and environmental triggers propelling individuals down this destructive path. From childhood trauma to unresolved intimacy issues, this subchapter delves into the complex web of factors that fuel phone sex addiction.

By shedding light on these root causes, practical strategies and tools are offered for breaking free from this addiction. Guidance is provided on seeking professional help, building healthy relationships, and discovering alternative outlets for sexual expression. Emphasis is placed on the importance of open communication, trust, and accountability in maintaining healthy relationships during the process of recovery.

Ultimately, "Unveiling the Deep-Rooted Causes of Phone Sex Addiction" aspires to empower individuals grappling with this addiction, offering them not only hope but a tangible roadmap to recovery. It is our steadfast belief that through understanding and addressing these root causes, individuals can emancipate themselves from the clutches of phone sex addiction, embarking on a transformative journey of healing, self-discovery, and embracing healthy sexual expression.

Strategic Approaches for Liberation: Overcoming the Shackles of Phone Sex Addiction

Phone sex addiction stands as a complex issue, casting its shadow upon individuals wrestling with various forms of sexual addiction, including online sex addiction, porn addiction, and cybersex addiction. In the subchapter titled "Strategic Approaches for Liberation: Overcoming the Shackles of Phone Sex Addiction," we embark on an exploration of effective methods and techniques, providing a roadmap for individuals to break free from this insidious habit and regain control over their lives.

1. Recognition and Acceptance: The inaugural step towards overcoming any addiction necessitates the acknowledgment of its existence. By recognizing phone sex addiction, individuals embark on the initial strides towards recovery.

2. Professional Guidance: Seeking the counsel of a qualified therapist or counselor specializing in sexual addiction becomes crucial. These professionals provide tailored guidance, unwavering support, and personalized treatment plans crafted to address the specific needs of the individual.

3. Establishment of Healthy Boundaries: The implementation of clear boundaries regarding phone and internet usage is imperative. Restricting access to phone sex at specific times and frequencies aids in regaining control and diminishes the urge for compulsive behavior.

4. Cultivation of Alternative Coping Mechanisms: Discovering healthy outlets for stress, anxiety, and boredom is pivotal. Engagement in activities such as exercise, hobbies, or quality time with loved ones offers alternative sources of pleasure and satisfaction.

5. *Mindfulness and Self-Awareness Practices:* Developing an understanding of the triggers that propel phone sex addiction requires mindfulness techniques and self-reflection. By practicing awareness, individuals can identify emotional states and redirect their energy towards healthier choices.

6. *Formation of a Support Network:* Encircling oneself with a supportive group of friends, family, or fellow recovering addicts is paramount. This network provides encouragement, accountability, and a safe space for sharing experiences.

7. *Wise Utilization of Technology:* Leveraging digital tools and apps designed to limit access to explicit content proves beneficial. Installation of filters and blockers that restrict access to adult websites or apps serves as a practical means to reduce temptation.

8. *Engagement in Therapy and Support Groups:* Participation in group therapy sessions or joining support groups dedicated to sex addiction fosters a sense of community. These environments allow individuals to share experiences, learn from others, and receive ongoing support.

9. Prioritization of Self-Care: Placing emphasis on self-care activities, including sufficient sleep, healthy eating, and regular exercise, is vital. These practices contribute to the maintenance of physical and mental well-being essential for long-term recovery.

10. Commitment and Patience: Overcoming phone sex addiction is an arduous process demanding time, effort, and dedication. A steadfast commitment to the journey of recovery, coupled with patience and self-compassion, proves integral.

Through the implementation of these strategies, individuals grappling with phone sex addiction can emancipate themselves from its grip, reclaiming agency over their lives. It is imperative to remember that recovery is not only possible but achievable, and with the right tools and support, individuals can overcome this addiction, sculpting a future marked by health and fulfillment.

Revitalizing Authentic Intimacy and Connection in the Digital Age: A Restorative Journey for Relationships

In an era dominated by technology, our relationships have undergone a profound transformation, marked by complexity and distance. The advent of technology has ushered in a new wave of addictions, contributing to the erosion of authentic intimacy and connection. In this subchapter, we embark on an exploration of the essential steps required to revitalize these foundational aspects in relationships marred by the shadows of sex addiction, porn addiction, and infidelity.

For those grappling with sex addiction, the allure of online sex, cybersex, and phone sex can be overpowering. These addictive behaviors often culminate in a detachment from reality, resulting in a breakdown of genuine intimacy. It becomes imperative for individuals to recognize the deleterious effects of these behaviors and initiate steps to break free from the cycle of addiction.

One of the initial steps towards revitalizing

authentic intimacy involves acknowledging the impact of these addictions on both oneself and one's partner. This necessitates honest and open communication, seeking professional help, and creating a safe space for both partners to express their emotions. By addressing the root causes of these addictive behaviors, individuals can commence the journey of healing and rebuilding trust within their relationships.

In instances of porn addiction, compulsive masturbation, and prostitution addiction, individuals may find themselves emotionally and physically detached from their partners. The revival of authentic intimacy requires a commitment to breaking free from these harmful behaviors and active engagement with one's partner. This engagement may involve the exploration of healthier sexual experiences together, fostering open communication about desires and boundaries, and discovering alternative avenues to fulfill emotional and physical needs.

For individuals who have succumbed to infidelity, revitalizing authentic intimacy becomes a nuanced and complex process, demanding introspection and a genuine willingness to change. Understanding the root causes behind the infidelity and addressing any unresolved issues within the relationship form the cornerstone of this journey. Rebuilding trust is a time-intensive process, demanding patience and consistent effort from both partners.

Ultimately, the revitalization of authentic intimacy and connection in relationships touched by various forms of sexual addiction requires a commitment to self-reflection, open communication, and professional support. By breaking free from addictive behaviors and actively engaging with one's partner, individuals can lay the groundwork for trust, emotional intimacy, and connection that fortify their relationships, fostering enduring fulfillment.

9

Overcoming Voyeurism Addiction

Unraveling the Complex Tapestry of Voyeurism Addiction

Voyeurism addiction, often relegated to the periphery of sexual addiction discussions, stands as a complex and frequently misunderstood facet of this intricate issue. While society may casually dismiss voyeurism as a harmless curiosity, it has the potential to swiftly evolve into an all-encompassing compulsion that disrupts relationships and personal well-being. In this subchapter, we embark on an in-depth exploration of the intricacies surrounding voyeurism addiction, aiming to cast light on its causes, consequences, and the potential pathways to recovery.

At its core, voyeurism addiction involves the pursuit of sexual pleasure derived from surreptitiously observing others without their knowledge or consent. Individuals grappling with this addiction often find themselves drawn to clandestine behaviors, such as peering through windows, consuming explicit content online, or even spying on unsuspecting individuals in public spaces. The allure of voyeurism lies in the thrill of the forbidden and the intricate power dynamics it elicits.

For those entangled in the web of sex addiction, voyeurism becomes a coping mechanism—a temporary escape from real-life problems or emotional voids. The act of observing others provides a momentary reprieve from personal insecurities or relationship challenges, offering a distorted sense of connection and arousal. However, as with any addiction, the consequences can be profound.

Engaging in voyeuristic behaviors can exact

severe repercussions for individuals and their relationships. The perpetual need for secrecy and deception corrodes trust, paving the way for feelings of guilt, shame, and isolation. Intimate relationships bear the brunt as the voyeur becomes increasingly preoccupied with their addictive behaviors, neglecting the emotional and physical needs of their partner.

Breaking free from the clutches of voyeurism addiction necessitates a multi-faceted approach that addresses both the underlying causes and the addictive behaviors themselves. Therapy, support groups, and specialized treatment programs emerge as invaluable tools, equipping individuals with the means to delve into the root causes of their addiction, develop healthier coping mechanisms, and rebuild trust within their relationships.

It is crucial for those grappling with voyeurism addiction to internalize the fact that recovery is not only a possibility but an achievable reality. By seeking help and confronting the intricate complexities of their addiction, individuals can initiate the reclamation of their lives, relationships, and sexual well-being. Through compassion, understanding, and a resolute commitment to personal growth, individuals can emancipate themselves from the chains of voyeurism addiction and embark on a transformative journey toward a healthier, more fulfilling future.

This subchapter aspires to illuminate the intricate nuances of voyeurism addiction, offering profound insight, unwavering support, and a beacon of hope for those ensnared in its grip. By recognizing the destructive nature of this addiction and actively seeking the necessary help, individuals can reclaim agency over their lives, fostering not only healthy relationships but also a reconnection with their authentic selves.

Navigating the Delicate Balance of Privacy and Consent in Voyeurism

Voyeurism, an intricately woven aspect of the realm of sexual addiction, intertwines with themes of invasion of privacy and the pivotal concept of consent. For individuals entangled in the intricate web of sex addiction, online sex addiction, porn addiction, cybersex addiction, and other related issues, comprehending the nuanced dynamics of voyeurism becomes paramount. This subchapter endeavors to illuminate these themes, offering valuable insights for individuals seeking liberation from phone sex addiction and its correlated behaviors.

Defined as the act of deriving sexual pleasure from observing others without their knowledge or consent, voyeurism, in essence, amounts to a breach of privacy and personal boundaries. It is imperative to recognize that engaging in voyeuristic behaviors without explicit consent is not only ethically questionable but also holds legal ramifications in many jurisdictions. Grasping the legal and ethical implications of voyeurism stands as a crucial step for those wrestling with sexual addiction within relationships.

Consent, a cornerstone principle in the realm of healthy sexual interactions, assumes heightened importance. It is essential for individuals to understand that consent must be explicit, enthusiastic, and ongoing. Unlike other realms of sexual expression, consent in voyeurism is an impossibility, as the act revolves around observing others without their knowledge or approval.

For individuals grappling with voyeurism addiction, recognizing the harm caused to others through the invasion of their privacy becomes a pivotal step toward recovery and personal growth. Developing empathy and understanding the negative consequences of voyeuristic behaviors can serve as a catalyst for individuals to break free from the cycle of addiction and transition into healthier, more respectful relationships.

In conclusion, comprehending the intricacies of invasion of privacy and the absence of consent in voyeurism is paramount for individuals navigating various forms of sexual addiction. Acknowledging the legal and ethical implications of voyeuristic behaviors, alongside understanding the critical role of consent, paves the way for fostering not just healthy relationships but also for the cultivation of respectful and consensual connections. By delving into these concepts, individuals can take tangible steps toward liberation from phone sex addiction, online sex addiction, porn addiction, and related issues.

Embarking on the Path of Recovery: Seeking Professional Help for Voyeurism Addiction

Voyeurism addiction, a labyrinthine and deeply entrenched issue, casts a shadow of detrimental effects on both the individual ensnared by the addiction and their relationships. If you find yourself perpetually compelled to spy on others without their consent, acknowledging the problem is the initial crucial step, followed by seeking professional help to extricate yourself from this harmful behavior.

Professional assistance proves indispensable in addressing voyeurism addiction, providing a structured and supportive environment for individuals to navigate the underlying causes of their addiction. Trained therapists specializing in sexual addiction bring valuable insights and guidance to the recovery process. They aid in understanding the root causes of voyeuristic tendencies, such as unresolved trauma, low self-esteem, or a need for control, and collaborate with individuals to develop healthier coping mechanisms.

Therapists deploy various evidence-based treatments to effectively address voyeurism addiction. Cognitive-behavioral therapy (CBT) emerges as a potent tool, facilitating the identification and challenge of distorted thoughts and beliefs associated with voyeurism, leading to the establishment of healthier behavioral patterns. Dialectical behavior therapy (DBT) plays a crucial role in managing intense emotions, enhancing interpersonal skills, and fostering impulse control. Group therapy sessions offer a supportive community where individuals can share experiences, struggles, and progress.

It is paramount to acknowledge that seeking professional help for voyeurism addiction does not promise an immediate or effortless recovery.

Breaking free from this addiction demands commitment, self-reflection, and a willingness to change. However, armed with the right support system and therapeutic interventions, overcoming voyeurism addiction is indeed a conceivable reality.

For those concerned about the impact of voyeurism addiction on their relationships, therapy can concurrently address the underlying issues that may have contributed to infidelity or dishonesty. Relationship counseling becomes instrumental in rebuilding trust, improving communication, and fostering a healthier intimate partnership where both parties feel understood and valued.

Remember, seeking professional help is an audacious and proactive step toward reclaiming a healthy and fulfilling life. By confronting voyeurism addiction, individuals can cast off the detrimental patterns that have held them back, cultivating healthier relationships built on trust, respect, and consent.

Crafting Robust Foundations: Nurturing Healthy Boundaries and Respect in Modern Relationships

As we navigate the digital landscape in the contemporary era, where technology seamlessly intertwines with our daily lives, relationships, too, undergo significant transformations. The ubiquity of connectivity has ushered in a new era of possibilities and challenges, particularly for individuals contending with sex addiction, online sex addiction, porn addiction, cybersex addiction, compulsive masturbation, prostitution addiction, exhibitionism addiction, phone sex addiction, voyeurism addiction, or any other manifestation of sexual addiction. These advancements, while offering myriad avenues for sexual activity and exploration through digital platforms, pose a distinct set of challenges for those ensnared in the complexities of addiction.

The subchapter titled "Nurturing Healthy Boundaries and Respect in Relationships," nestled within the book "Dialing Desire: Breaking Free from Phone Sex Addiction," assumes a crucial role in providing guidance and support to those entangled in addictive behaviors and ensnared in tumultuous relationships. Specifically tailored for an audience grappling with sex addiction, porn addiction, and infidelity, this chapter recognizes the distinctive struggles faced by individuals traversing these challenging terrains.

The chapter initiates its exploration by underscoring the paramount importance of establishing healthy boundaries in relationships. It delves into the nuanced concept of consent, urging readers to prioritize open and transparent communication with their partners. By actively setting and respecting boundaries, individuals can cultivate a safe and secure environment wherein both parties can thrive and flourish.

Respect, another pivotal component of nurturing healthy relationships, receives meticulous attention. The chapter unfurls a comprehensive discussion on the significance of respect for oneself and for others, emphasizing the profound importance of treating one's partner with dignity and kindness. It delves into the detrimental consequences of objectification, encouraging readers to perceive their partners as equals rather than mere objects of desire.

Moreover, the subchapter proffers practical tips and strategies for fostering respect and healthy boundaries within relationships. It imparts guidance on effective communication, proposes trust-building exercises, and advocates for the exploration of shared interests and values. Additionally, it serves as a repository of resources, offering suggestions for seeking professional help, such as therapy or support groups, to facilitate the arduous journey toward recovery.

"Nurturing Healthy Boundaries and Respect in Relationships" emerges as a beacon for individuals wrestling with sexual addiction in relationships. By championing the cause of healthy boundaries and respect, this subchapter endeavors to empower individuals to extricate themselves from destructive patterns, fostering not only healthy but also meaningful connections with their partners. Through these foundational principles, it paves the way for individuals to break free from the shackles of addiction and forge a path toward enduring fulfillment and genuine connection.

10

Navigating Sexual Addiction in Relationships

The Profound Impact of Sexual Addiction on Partners and Relationships

Sexual addiction, a multifaceted and often misconstrued condition, possesses the potential for profound repercussions on both the individual entangled in its grip and their partners. Within the confines of this subchapter, our endeavor is to meticulously dissect the detrimental impact of sexual addiction on partners and relationships, casting a discerning light on the myriad challenges faced by those ensnared in this complex web.

Partners of individuals grappling with sex addiction frequently find themselves in the throes of significant emotional distress, besieged by sensations of betrayal, hurt, and confusion stemming from their loved one's actions. A poignant cascade of emotions, including feelings of low self-worth and inadequacy, tends to pervade their psyche, prompting an unsettling introspection into their own desirability. The very foundation of any meaningful relationship—trust—stands shattered, leaving partners teetering on the precipice of constant suspicion and an unrelenting fear of further betrayal.

The addictive behaviors intertwined with sexual addiction, be it compulsive masturbation, online sexual encounters, consumption of explicit content, or involvement in prostitution, metamorphose into a wedge driving itself between partners. The delicate threads of intimacy and emotional connection fray as the addict becomes increasingly ensnared in the labyrinth of their compulsions, diverting attention from the needs of their partner. This erosion often manifests as a breakdown in communication, a void of emotional support, and an overall disintegration of the fabric binding the relationship.

Sexual addiction invariably coexists with secrecy and deception, manifesting in hidden online profiles, clandestine explicit messages, or the unearthing of evidence pointing to infidelity. The revelation of these concealed truths unfurls a maelstrom of pain and anger, culminating in a loss of respect and a profound sense of betrayal that further corrodes the emotional bond between partners.

Tragically, sexual addiction can transcend the boundaries of emotional infidelity, driving the addict to seek fulfillment beyond the confines of the relationship. This not only jeopardizes the health and safety of the addict but also exposes their unsuspecting partners to potential sexually transmitted infections and the enduring trauma of emotional discord.

Moreover, sexual addiction assumes the insidious guise of a financial strain within the relationship. The addict may recklessly expend excessive sums on pornography, phone sex services, or even prostitution, catalyzing financial discord that escalates into arguments, resentment, and a further deterioration of the relational landscape.

Addressing the deleterious impact of sexual addiction on partners and relationships necessitates the embrace of a comprehensive approach. Therapy, whether individual or couples counseling, emerges as a linchpin for the rebuilding of trust, the establishment of healthy boundaries, and the amelioration of communication. Support groups, specifically tailored for partners of sex addicts, serve as sanctuaries for shared experiences and invaluable insights, fostering a collective journey toward healing.

By acknowledging the profound impact of sexual addiction on partners and relationships, individuals grappling with these issues can embark on the necessary path toward healing. Armed with the tools to reconstruct their lives and rebuild connections with their loved ones, the journey of recovery becomes a beacon of hope and restoration.

Navigating the Maze of Communication: Addressing Sexual Addiction in Relationships

Sexual addiction, a force capable of unsettling the very foundations of relationships, leaves in its wake trust issues, emotional turbulence, and a pervasive sense of dissatisfaction. To navigate this intricate terrain, effective communication strategies emerge as indispensable. This subchapter aspires to serve as a guiding light, offering counsel on how individuals wrestling with sexual addiction can initiate communication with their partners, surmount obstacles, and embark on the arduous journey of rebuilding trust.

1. Open and Honest Communication:

The bedrock of any flourishing relationship lies in open and honest communication. It is imperative for individuals contending with sexual addiction to articulate their struggles, emotions, and desires transparently to their partners. This candid dialogue serves as the embryonic stage of a collective healing process.

2. Active Listening:

Partners of individuals ensnared in the throes of sex addiction require a secure space to voice their concerns, fears, and emotions. By engaging in active listening—providing undivided attention, validating feelings, and refraining from judgment—those grappling with addiction can manifest their commitment to change and set the wheels of trust rebuilding in motion.

3. Establishing Boundaries:

In the realm of relationships tainted by sexual addiction, delineating clear boundaries proves to be a non-negotiable imperative. These boundaries extend to defining acceptable and unacceptable parameters concerning sexual behavior, online activities, and external relationships. Openly engaging in this dialogue not only fosters trust but also lays the groundwork for a secure environment conducive to recovery.

4. Seeking Professional Help:

Sexual addiction, with its labyrinthine complexities, frequently demands professional intervention. Couples therapy or individual counseling provides a neutral and safe haven to unravel the layers of addiction, address underlying issues, and forge a path toward healing. Opting for professional help serves as a testament to the commitment to personal growth and the preservation of the relationship.

5. Developing Healthy Coping Mechanisms:

The journey toward overcoming sexual addiction necessitates the active cultivation of healthier coping mechanisms. Encouraging partners to partake in activities promoting self-care—be it exercise, hobbies, or quality time together—contributes to the attenuation of reliance on addictive behaviors.

6. Rebuilding Trust:

Rebuilding trust post-sexual addiction is akin to navigating uncharted waters. It demands patience, consistency, and accountability. Accepting responsibility for actions, demonstrating genuine remorse, and following through with commitments form the scaffolding for the gradual reconstruction of trust.

Conclusion:

Addressing sexual addiction within relationships demands a nuanced and multifaceted approach, with effective communication strategies occupying a central role. Through the channels of open dialogue, active listening, boundary establishment, professional intervention, the cultivation of healthy coping mechanisms, and the gradual rebuilding of trust, individuals struggling with sexual addiction and their partners can embark on a journey of recovery. It is a process that unfolds over time, necessitating effort and dedication, but armed with these communication strategies, a relationship characterized by fulfillment and health is indeed within reach.

Embarking on the Path of Healing:

Rebuilding Trust and Intimacy Post-Sexual Addiction

Embarking on the path of recovery from sexual addiction is an odyssey fraught with challenges, demanding unwavering dedication and profound commitment. At the epicenter of this transformative journey lies the pivotal task of rebuilding trust and intimacy with one's partner. Within this subchapter, we delve into effective strategies and techniques, guiding individuals ensnared in the clutches of sex addiction, porn addiction, or infidelity in regaining trust and fostering healthy intimacy in their relationships.

1. Open and Honest Communication:

The cornerstone of trust restoration is the cultivation of open and honest communication. Initiating sincere conversations with one's partner about the intricacies of addiction, the nuances of the recovery process, and a genuine commitment to change sets the stage for shared healing.

2. Seeking Professional Help:

Navigating the complexities of sexual addiction often requires the skilled guidance of a professional.

Engaging in therapy or counseling, particularly with a qualified sex addiction specialist, provides a structured platform to explore underlying issues, develop healthier coping mechanisms, and establish clear boundaries within the relationship. Professional help becomes a beacon, illuminating the path toward recovery.

3. Consistency and Accountability:

Rebuilding trust is an incremental process necessitating unwavering consistency and accountability. Actions must align with commitments, and acknowledgment of responsibility for past transgressions becomes a cornerstone in demonstrating genuine efforts toward change.

4. Patience and Understanding:

Healing is a nuanced process, and partners often traverse a landscape of complex emotions, ranging from anger to betrayal. Practicing patience, empathy, and understanding is paramount, allowing partners the time they need to heal and re-establish trust.

5. Re-establishing Intimacy:

Sexual addiction has an insidious effect on intimacy, requiring a delicate and gradual reestablishment. Focusing on emotional connection, vulnerability, and rebuilding the emotional bond precedes any foray into sexual activities. Exploring new avenues to express love and affection becomes a transformative element in breaking free from addictive patterns.

6. Creating a Supportive Environment:

Enveloping oneself in a supportive community, comprising individuals who understand the struggles associated with addiction, fosters resilience and motivation. Support groups and online forums provide valuable spaces for shared experiences, insights, and encouragement throughout the process of rebuilding trust and intimacy.

Rebuilding trust and intimacy post-sexual addiction is a formidable but achievable pursuit. Armed with these strategies, coupled with professional help, individuals can forge a path toward a relationship characterized by health, trust, and mutual respect.

Sustaining the Flame: Nurturing

Healthy Sexual Dynamics in Long-Term Relationships

In the intricate tapestry of long-term relationships, sustaining a healthy and satisfying sexual dynamic emerges as a nuanced challenge. This subchapter assumes the mantle of a guide, offering insights and practical advice tailored for individuals grappling with a spectrum of sexual addictions within the context of committed relationships.

Understanding the profound impact of addictive behaviors on intimate connections serves as the foundational stepping stone toward healing. It necessitates a compassionate exploration of the underlying factors contributing to these patterns that have the potential to jeopardize trust, stir feelings of betrayal, induce isolation, and erode self-esteem.

Sustaining healthy sexual dynamics mandates the cultivation of open and honest communication between partners. Facilitating a dialogue surrounding desires, boundaries, and expectations creates a safe haven for both individuals to articulate their needs and concerns. Developing effective communication skills, such as active listening and empathy, serves not only to rebuild trust but also to fortify the emotional connection.

Professional help, in the form of therapy or counseling, emerges as an integral component of the recovery process. A qualified therapist guides individuals and couples in unraveling the layers of addiction, addressing underlying issues, and developing healthier coping mechanisms. Through this therapeutic journey, partners can collaboratively rebuild intimacy and establish new behavioral patterns prioritizing mutual respect and consent.

Engaging in self-care practices assumes equal importance in sustaining healthy sexual dynamics. This entails nurturing physical, emotional, and mental well-being through regular exercise, a balanced diet, and prioritizing quality sleep. Exploring alternative outlets for stress, such as meditation or creative hobbies, offers healthier avenues to cope with triggers or cravings.

Cultivating a support network of understanding and non-judgmental individuals becomes a powerful antidote to the shame and isolation often associated with addictive behaviors. Participating in support groups or seeking online communities provides a space for shared experiences, insights, and encouragement from others who have faced similar challenges.

In conclusion, sustaining healthy sexual dynamics in long-term relationships mandates dedication, understanding, and a commitment to personal growth. By addressing the underlying factors contributing to addictive behaviors, fostering open communication, seeking professional help, practicing self-care, and building a supportive network, individuals can break free from their patterns of addiction, cultivating fulfilling and intimate connections with their partners.

11

Embracing a Life Free from Sexual Addiction

Embarking on the Profound Journey to Recovery and Healing

In the enthralling subchapter titled "The Journey to Recovery and Healing" within the transformative narrative of "Dialing Desire: Breaking Free from Phone Sex Addiction," we embark on an odyssey of profound significance. This chapter stands as a dedicated guide for those grappling with sex addiction, porn addiction, infidelity, and a spectrum of sexual compulsions, including online sex

addiction, cybersex addiction, compulsive masturbation, prostitution addiction, exhibitionism addiction, phone sex addiction, voyeurism addiction,
and the intricate dynamics of sexual addiction
within relationships.

The trajectory of recovery from any form of
addiction is marked by challenges, empowerment,
and the undeniable need for self-reflection. It is a
voyage that demands an unwavering commitment
to confront the root causes of our addictive behaviors. Within the pages of this subchapter, we
endeavor to unravel the path to healing, weaving
together profound insights, actionable guidance,
and practical tools to illuminate your journey toward recovery.

The initial stride on this transformative journey is the courageous acknowledgment of the
problem's existence and its profound impact on
personal life and relationships. By deciphering the
destructive patterns, a doorway to change swings
open, fostering the potential for a rebirth. We
embark on a deep exploration of the underlying

psychological, emotional, and social factors intricately woven into the tapestry of sexual addiction, facilitating a profound understanding of the individual struggles one faces.

Subsequently, we traverse the expansive landscape of therapeutic approaches available for recovery. From the intimacy of individual therapy to the communal embrace of support groups, we delve into the nuanced benefits of each method, offering advice on discovering the right professional support uniquely tailored to individual needs. The narrative underscores the importance of constructing a support network, intertwining stories of shared experiences and triumphs that serve as beacons of hope.

Woven through the fabric of this chapter are practical strategies meticulously designed to guide you through the labyrinth of triggers and cravings. We explore the terrain of healthy coping mechanisms, from the meditative embrace of mindfulness to the invigorating realms of exercise and the cathartic release found in creative pursuits. By embracing these transformative techniques, you will gradually reclaim control over your thoughts and actions, paving the way for a profound healing process.

Moreover, we address the unique challenges faced by individuals entangled in relationships affected by sexual addiction. Offering sage advice on rebuilding trust, fostering open communication, and establishing healthy boundaries, we underscore the reality that healing is a collective endeavor—one that seeks reconciliation with those who may have been unintentionally hurt along the way.

In the pages of "The Journey to Recovery and Healing," we present a roadmap to liberation from the insidious clutches of addiction. Infused with personal narratives, expert insights, and practical exercises, this subchapter stands as a guiding beacon—offering not only hope and inspiration but also a meticulously charted course toward a life characterized by fulfillment, free from the shackles of sexual addiction. Remember, the prospect of recovery is tangible, and together, we forge ahead to break free from the vice-like grip of sexual addiction.

Nurturing the Seeds of Self-Compassion and Forgiveness

In the profound journey of breaking free from phone sex addiction, it is incumbent not only to unravel the root causes and seek professional help but also to cultivate the seeds of self-compassion and forgiveness. This subchapter is a compassionate guide for sex addicts, porn addicts, and those who have grappled with infidelity, as it unfolds the delicate process of nurturing these essential qualities.

Self-compassion, a practice steeped in treating oneself with kindness, understanding, and empathy, emerges as a cornerstone in the voyage of those grappling with sex addiction. It entails acknowledging one's struggles without the harsh glare of judgment or self-criticism. For those ensnared in the labyrinth of sex addiction, it is paramount to grasp that this intricate issue is deeply rooted in psychological, emotional, and social complexities. Cultivating self-compassion becomes the catalyst for forgiving oneself for past actions, paving the way for a focused journey of healing and self-improvement.

To foster self-compassion, the narrative encourages self-reflection and the gentle challenge of negative self-talk. An understanding is fostered that addiction is not an individual's defining characteristic but rather a condition that can be surmounted with concerted effort and support. The practice of self-care is spotlighted, urging individuals to engage in activities that foster emotional well-being, such as exercise, meditation, or journaling. The importance of weaving a supportive network, comprised of friends, family, or support groups, surfaces as an invaluable resource, offering understanding and encouragement throughout the arduous journey of recovery.

Parallel to the cultivation of self-compassion, the subchapter unfurls the tapestry of forgiveness—a pivotal aspect of healing from addiction.

This transformative process involves the delicate act of releasing resentment and anger toward oneself and others. For those who have traversed the fraught terrain of infidelity, the acknowledgment of pain and betrayal becomes a necessary prelude to the crucial step of forgiveness—an indispensable facet of personal growth and relationship repair.

The cultivation of forgiveness, the narrative posits, requires open and honest communication with partners, potentially seeking professional guidance to navigate the intricate nuances of healing. The onus lies on taking responsibility for past actions, expressing genuine remorse, and demonstrating a steadfast commitment to change. Infusing empathy into this process, both toward oneself and others, is underscored as a transformative element in fostering a more forgiving mindset.

It is imperative to recognize that the nurturing of self-compassion and forgiveness is a gradual journey, one that demands patience and unwavering persistence. Setbacks are acknowledged as a natural part of the process, but armed with the right support and mindset, the prospect of recovery remains tangible.

By embracing the virtues of self-compassion and forgiveness, individuals catapult themselves toward liberation from the cyclical grip of phone sex addiction, porn addiction, and infidelity. The journey unfolds as one of self-discovery, healing, and personal growth—a trajectory that leads not only to healthier relationships but also to a life steeped in fulfillment and authenticity.

Cultivating a Resilient Support Network and Robust Accountability System

In the intricate tapestry of breaking free from phone sex addiction, the realization dawns: you are not alone in this challenging journey. A myriad of individuals, much like yourself, grapple with a spectrum of sexual addictions—online sex addiction, porn addiction, cybersex addiction, and more. Acknowledging and accepting this shared reality is the inaugural step toward healing and recovery.

Central to this journey is the cultivation of a resilient support network—an ensemble of individuals who intimately understand the labyrinthine struggles inherent to sexual addiction. Enveloping oneself in the compassionate embrace of people who provide non-judgmental support, guidance, and encouragement becomes a cornerstone of the recovery process. The narrative advocates for the active pursuit of support groups, therapy sessions, or online communities dedicated to sex addiction. In these spaces, individuals can share their experiences, lend a listening ear, and glean wisdom from those who have navigated similar challenges.

In tandem with personal support, the narrative illuminates the importance of accountability—an indispensable facet of overcoming addiction. This involves a conscious undertaking of responsibility for one's actions and an active commitment to transformation. Establishing a robust accountability system offers structure and guidance, ensuring individuals stay on course. This system may include regular check-ins with a trusted friend, family member, or therapist—opportunities for open discussions about progress, setbacks, and aspirations. The act of sharing one's struggles and triumphs with an accountability partner fosters a profound sense of commitment and serves as a motivational force in staying focused on the recovery journey.

Acknowledging the dual nature of technology in the journey of overcoming sexual addiction, the narrative elucidates its potential as both a boon and a challenge. While the internet and smartphones can be triggers for addictive behaviors, they also offer valuable tools for recovery. Suggestions include the utilization of apps or software designed to monitor and limit internet usage, block explicit content, or track progress. These technological aids can assist in fostering a healthier relationship with technology and mitigating the risk of relapse.

It is paramount to internalize that overcoming addiction is an intricate process—one that demands patience, resilience, and self-compassion.

Surrounded by a supportive network and fortified by an accountability system, individuals find themselves on a trajectory toward success. Embracing the opportunity to learn from the experiences of others, sharing personal narratives, and collectively growing become integral components of this transformative journey.

By actively seeking and embracing support, individuals exhibit a courageous stride toward breaking free from the chains of phone sex addiction. In this collective endeavor, the refrain echoes: You are not alone, and the prospect of a brighter, healthier future is not only conceivable but distinctly attainable.

Envisioning a Life of Wholesome and Gratifying Sexual Expression

In the contemporary era dominated by technology, where our lives are intricately interwoven with digital threads, it comes as no surprise that our experiences of sexuality have evolved. Yet, for individuals ensnared in the throes of addictive behaviors—sex addiction, online sex addiction, porn addiction, cybersex addiction, compulsive masturbation, prostitution addiction, exhibitionism addiction, phone sex addiction, voyeurism addiction, or sexual addiction within relationships—the pursuit of a fulfilling and healthy sexual lifestyle may seem like an elusive aspiration.

"Dialing Desire: Breaking Free from Phone Sex Addiction" emerges as a comprehensive guide, a beacon of hope for sex addicts, porn addicts, and those who have grappled with infidelity. This subchapter, titled "Embracing a Fulfilling and Healthy Sexual Lifestyle," dives deep into the vital strategies and insights that empower individuals to liberate themselves from addictive patterns and nurture a balanced and gratifying sexual life.

Immersed within these pages is a treasure trove of information and practical advice, meticulously crafted to address the unique needs of those embroiled in the complexity of addiction. The book, cognizant of the intricate layers of addiction and its impact on sexual behaviors, unfurls a roadmap toward healing and transformation. It delves into the underlying psychological, emotional, and societal factors that contribute to addictive behaviors while offering actionable techniques for overcoming them.

Embark on the journey to embrace a fulfilling and healthy sexual lifestyle by:

1. Understanding the Root Causes:

Unearth the profound reasons behind addictive behaviors, exploring topics such as childhood trauma, intimacy issues, and the influence of cultural and societal norms.

2. Developing Self-Awareness:

Gain profound insights into triggers, cravings, and emotional patterns, empowering yourself to recognize and interrupt destructive behaviors before they escalate.

3. Establishing Boundaries:

Learn the art of setting clear boundaries in relationships and sexual encounters, fostering mutual respect and safeguarding your overall well-being.

4. Building Healthy Connections:

Cultivate meaningful and intimate connections

with others, be it in romantic relationships or through support groups, as a potent antidote to feelings of isolation and shame.

5. Exploring Alternative Outlets:

Discover healthier avenues to satisfy your sexual desires, engaging in creative activities, exercise, mindfulness practices, or exploring non-sexual hobbies.

6. Seeking Professional Help:

Acknowledge the pivotal role of therapy, counseling, and support groups in your journey, recognizing the invaluable guidance, accountability, and safe space they provide for healing.

By embracing a fulfilling and healthy sexual lifestyle, you liberate yourself from the clutches of addiction, crafting a future adorned with genuine connections, self-acceptance, and sexual fulfillment. "Dialing Desire: Breaking Free from Phone Sex Addiction" serves as your guide, empowering you to reclaim control over your sexuality and unfold a life imbued with joy, authenticity, and meaningful relationships.

12

Living a Life of Liberation and Authenticity

Embarking on the Transformative Odyssey Towards Liberation from Phone Sex Addiction

In our odyssey to break free from the clutches of phone sex addiction, we've meticulously explored the intricate facets of our lives ensnared by this pernicious behavior. From the magnetic allure of online sex addiction to the intricate labyrinth of pornography and the deleterious impact of compulsive masturbation, we've delved deep into the multifaceted complexities of sexual addiction in the digital age. Our journey has led us through the shadows of prostitution, exhibitionism, voyeurism, and the profound repercussions these addictive behaviors cast upon the canvas of our relationships.

Yet, amidst the profound darkness that addiction often begets, there is a beacon of hope illuminating our path. The trajectory toward liberation and authenticity commences with a profound acknowledgment of our addiction and the far-reaching consequences it imposes upon our lives. It necessitates a courageous act of taking responsibility for our actions and making an unwavering commitment to change. It is only through this heightened self-awareness that the tapestry of healing can begin to unfurl.

Living a life defined by liberation and authenticity transcends the mere cessation of addictive behaviors. It beckons us to embrace our true selves, unshackled from the chains of addiction, and to forge meaningful connections grounded in trust, respect, and open communication. It calls us to be fully present in each moment, eschewing the allure of the virtual world as we navigate the uncharted waters of genuine human connection.

The journey to recovery from sex addiction is undeniably arduous, demanding unwavering dedication, relentless perseverance, and the scaffolding of a robust support system. Seeking professional help, whether through therapy or support groups, emerges as an invaluable compass guiding us through the turbulent seas of transformation. It is imperative to surround ourselves with empathetic individuals who not only comprehend our struggles but also provide a safe sanctuary for the candid sharing of our experiences.

True emancipation from the clutches of addiction mandates a holistic approach that extends beyond surface-level behavior modification. It compels us to excavate the underlying issues that act as the crucible for our desires—issues that may be rooted in past traumas, insecurities, or emotional vulnerabilities. By illuminating the shadowed recesses of our psyche and comprehending the root causes of our addiction, we pave the way for the development of healthier coping mechanisms and fortify our resilience against the siren call of future relapses.

Living a life characterized by liberation and authenticity does not translate to the suppression of natural instincts or the denial of our inherent sexual desires. Instead, it entails finding an equilibrium between our needs and our values. It beckons us to engage in healthy, consensual, respectful, and fulfilling sexual relationships that align with the core tenets of our authentic selves.

As we stand on the precipice of concluding this transformative journey, let us engrave in our consciousness the profound understanding that change is not only plausible but inherently attainable. Armed with the empowering realization that we possess the agency to reclaim our lives and reconstruct our relationships, we step forth into a future where seeking help, embracing our vulnerabilities, and committing to a life of authenticity become the guiding stars that lead us to break free from the suffocating chains of addiction. Through these deliberate actions, we rediscover the boundless joy and fulfillment that emanate from genuine human connection—the very essence that renders our existence truly authentic and liberated.